SUBMARINES &
SHIPS

RICHARD HUMBLE

HAMLYN

Acknowledgements

The publishers would like to thank Jonathan Adams, who illustrated the four see-through scenes and the heading icons; Gerald Wood, who illustrated the cover; and the organizations and individuals who have given their permission to reproduce the pictures in this book:

Ancient Art & Architecture Collection/Ronald Sheridan: 9.
Archiv fur Kunst und Geschichte/Erich Lessing: 7, 42 left.
Bibliotheque Nationale, Paris: 15.
Bridgeman Art Library/Lambeth Palace Library: 21 top left,
/National Maritime Museum 26 top, /Bonhams, London 29 top.
The British Library: 19 (Royal 10e iv f19). **Christie's Images:** 27 bottom.
Department of Defense, Still Media Records Center/Gallagher Phan: 45.
Mary Evans Picture Library: 34, 41.
Michael Holford: 4, /British Museum 6, /Museum vor Volkekunde, Munich 11,
/Musee de Bayeux 13, /Science Museum 21 bottom left, /Science Museum 21 right,
/Science Museum 22.
Robert Hunt Library: 42 right, 43 bottom.
Richard Hunter: 36. **Imperial War Museum:** 43 top.
Kon-Tiki Museum, Oslo: 5. **National Maritime Museum, Antwerp:** 23.
National Maritime Museum, London: 25, 26 bottom, 27 top, 29 bottom.
Colin Martin: 24 top right. **The Mary Rose Trust:** 24 top left.
Photographie Giraudon/Reims Cathedral: 18.
Reed International Books Ltd/Mark R. Wallis: 30.
S.S. Great Britain/S.W.P.A: 31.
T.R.H./U.S. Navy: 35. **U.S. Navy**/E.J. Bonner: 39.
Werner Forman Archive/Statens Historiska Museum, Stockholm: 12.

Illustrators:
Jonathan Adams: 8-9, 16-17, 32-33, 40-41, heading icons.
Peter Bull Art: all maps.
Bill Donohoe: 4 bottom, 5, 34.
Nick Hewetson: 6-7, 14, 23 middle right, 43 bottom right, 46-47.
Christian Hook: 4 top left, 10-11 (both).
Jonathon Potter: 22, 30-31, 35, 44-45 (both).
Tony Townsend: 13 (bottom right), 15, 18, 21, 23 bottom, 28 top left, 29,
31 bottom right, 42-43 (main picture).
Paul Weston: 19, 27, 38-39 (both).
Gerald Wood: Cover, 12-13 (main picture), 20, 24, 25,
28 bottom, 36-37 (both).

Editor: Andrew Farrow
Designer: Anne Sharples
Picture Researchers: Judy Todd and Liz Fowler
Production Controllers: Mark Leonard and Christine Campbell

First published in Great Britain 1995
by Hamlyn Children's Books,
an imprint of Reed Children's Books,
Michelin House, 81 Fulham Road, London SW3 6RB,
and Auckland, Melbourne, Singapore and Toronto.

ISBN 0 600 58412 7

A CIP catalogue record for this book is available at the British Library.

Books printed and bound by Proost, Belgium

CONTENTS

Coracles (above) are very simple boats made from animal skins stretched over a bowl-shaped framework. They are very light and easy to carry. Dug-out canoes (top right) were first made about 10,000 years ago, in the Stone Age. They are made by carefully chipping away the centre of a heavy log. Sometimes the wood is burned away with a line of small fires.

L ong ago, before the first written records, early humans learned how to use floating materials such as logs, bundles of reeds and inflated animal skins to travel along rivers and across lakes. Then, over 5,000 years ago, people of the great civilizations of Egypt and Sumer built the first sail-powered ships and ventured into the open sea. In this book you will find out about some of the world's most important ships, and see how they developed from the first simple boats into the sophisticated ships that sail the oceans today.

THE FIRST BOATS

Boat-building is an ancient and important craft. It enabled people to travel without being hindered by rivers and lakes, to fish for food, and to make short voyages out to sea. Prehistoric boat-building almost certainly began with rafts (platforms of logs tied together with rope) and coracles (wooden frames covered with animal skins). They are both paddled, because neither is big enough to carry a mast, so they cannot be driven by a following wind. Coracles were probably first used for fishing in rivers and lakes, and are still used in several countries today.

Rafts are floating platforms made by lashing logs together side by side. Rafts can carry more passengers than dug-out canoes, but are much harder to paddle and steer.

This tomb-carving from about 2400 BC shows Egyptian shipbuilders at work. They are using adzes (a kind of axe) and chisels to smooth the planking of the ship's hollow hull. The hull planks were fastened together with wooden pegs.

REED BOATS

The earliest sea-going boats were built around 3,000 BC by the river peoples of Egypt, Sumer (now southern Iraq) and Mohenjo-Daro (Pakistan). These countries did not have trees from which long timbers could be cut for building large boats, but their rivers were densely fringed with papyrus reeds.

Egyptian carvings from 5,000 years ago show boat-builders expertly tying reeds into stiff bundles. These were then lashed together to form a hull curved upward at the bow (front) and stern (back). Small boats were driven and steered by paddles. Larger ones were steered by large oars at the stern, but carried a sail - a square piece of cloth - on a two-legged mast, to catch following winds.

TRADING BY SEA

The Sumerians and Egyptians soon began to use these ships for trade. This was because travelling by sea is usually quicker than travelling by land. Although few ships were seaworthy enough to venture far from land, the Egyptians were soon busy trading along the Mediterranean coast between the mouth of the River Nile and Lebanon. It was from Lebanon that Egypt imported cedar wood to build bigger and better ships.

THE OLDEST-KNOWN SHIP

With imported Lebanon cedar, the Egyptians built the oldest-known ship still in existence today. It was used only once, for the funeral of Pharaoh Khufu (Cheops), builder of the Great Pyramid, who ruled Egypt in about 2,600 BC.

This graceful craft is 51 metres long, and was rowed by 10 oars. It was taken to pieces and buried with the dead pharaoh. Some 4,500 years later, archaeologists discovered the ship and fitted together its 1,200 timbers - making it the world's oldest construction kit!

Thor Heyerdahl's ship Ra, *made of papyrus reed. Six years after his voyage on the* Ra, *Heyerdahl sailed a Sumerian-type reed ship, called* Tigris, *round Africa from Iraq to Somalia: a voyage of 6,750 kilometres in 144 days.*

The last voyage of a dead pharaoh. Although built with great craftsmanship, the elegant funeral ships of Ancient Egypt were designed only for the calm waters of the River Nile, not for voyages on the open sea.

RA AND TIGRIS

Modern experiments have proved that some Sumerian and Egyptian reed ships were actually capable of making long voyages on the open sea. In 1970, using the skills of African and South American peoples who still build reed boats, Norwegian adventurer Thor Heyerdahl built a reed ship 18 metres long and six metres wide. Heyerdahl's crew sailed this ship, named *Ra* after the Egyptian sun god, across the Atlantic Ocean. Setting out from Morocco in North Africa, *Ra* reached Barbados in the West Indies in 57 days.

FLEETS OF THE PHARAOHS

The Egyptian empire became the world's first sea power. From the evidence of pictures on tombs and monuments, we know that many Egyptian merchant ships sailed the eastern Mediterranean and down the Red Sea to bring home the riches of East Africa.

By the time of the Egyptian 'Middle Kingdom' (about 1991-1786 BC), ships and boats were so important in the life of Egypt that models of them were buried with the dead. The Egyptians believed that the dead would be able to use them in an afterlife. This model of an Egyptian sailing boat dates from about 1800 BC.

SHIPS FOR WAR OR PEACE

About a hundred years after the burial of Khufu's funeral ship, the Pharaoh Sahure sent a fleet of eight troop-carrying ships to attack the coast of Syria. To celebrate the success of the mission, the pharoah built a victory monument which was decorated with pictures of his ships. It clearly shows vessels which could carry cargo as well as troops. They could be rowed as well as sailed, with seven oars on each side. The two-legged mast carried a single square sail, and was lowered backwards onto a tall cradle when the ship was being rowed. There were six steering oars at the stern, three on each side.

TO THE 'LAND OF PUNT'

The powerful Queen Hatshepsut ruled Egypt from 1503-1482 BC. Her most famous monument is to a sea voyage, not of war but of peace. It shows ships from a trading fleet which sailed down the Red Sea to the 'Land of Punt' (probably modern Somalia, in East Africa). Each ship was much bigger than Sahure's warships, with twice as many oars (14 a side).

The hull was built up from a central backbone called a keel, which does not seem to have been a feature of earlier Egyptian ships. The keel gave the ship increased strength, and rose at either end to form a high bow and a gracefully curved stern. It supported a single fixed mast, which had replaced the two-legged collapsible mast of Sahure's ships.

This map shows the seas cruised by the sea-going reed ships of Sumer and the reed and wooden ships of Egypt: the Mediterranean and Red Seas, and south to the Indian Ocean and the coast of East Africa.

Egypt

Sumer

East Africa

INDIAN OCEAN

DECK-BEAMS AND RIGGING

Queen Hatshepsut's ships also had wooden beams across them, supporting the deck and bracing the sides of the ship together. This shows that there were probably large cargo holds below deck, and that these vessels were broader and stronger than earlier Egyptian ships. They were probably between 29 and 32 metres long, judging by the number of oars.

Apart from being stronger and more seaworthy, Queen Hatshepsut's ships were probably much easier to sail than those of Sahure's fleet. Details of their rigging clearly shows ropes that could be used for swinging the sail to catch changes in the wind direction.

RAMESSES III

Egypt's last great warrior pharaoh was Ramesses III (1198-1166 BC). During his reign, Egypt was attacked by enemies whom the Egyptians called the 'People from the Sea'. These were probably tribes driven south from Crete. Ramesses defeated them on land and at sea.

SEA BATTLES

Ramesses' tomb at Medinet Habu has the first-known pictures of a sea battle. It shows a type of warship which would be used in sea battles for the next 4,000 years: war galleys, built solely for fighting.

Galleys were narrow, lightly-built ships which had both sails and oars. They were sailed when looking for the enemy fleet, but rowed into battle. Their keel extended forward to form a pointed ram, strengthened with a heavy bronze animal-head, for smashing holes in enemy ships. When the galley had managed to hit an enemy ship, the rowers would then back the galley away before attacking the next ship. The galleys of Ramesses III also carried soldiers for boarding and capturing enemy vessels.

This relief from Queen Hatshepsut's tomb shows cargo-carrying ships from the trading fleet she sent to the East African 'Land of Punt'.

This reconstruction of one of the war galleys of Ramesses III shows its single fixed mast and the forward-jutting ram for smashing and sinking enemy ships in battle. The galleys each had a single steering oar.

GREECE AND ROME

In the see-through scene below, two large merchant ships are loading and unloading their cargoes, which include grain and wild animals. Rome had to import huge quantities of grain from the provinces it had conquered, like Egypt, or her hungry citizens would riot. Ships also brought wild animals such as lions and tigers from Africa and India. Gladiators, criminals and sometimes Christians had to fight the animals to entertain the people at the great Games held throughout the Empire.

After the decline of the Egyptian empire, Phoenicia (now part of Syria) and Greece emerged as the next great sea powers. However, they in turn were eclipsed by the might of the Romans.

GALLEYS

The Phoenicians' rise to power began around 1100 BC. They protected their merchant fleets with war galleys. So did their rivals in southern Europe, the city-states of Greece. The first Greek galleys had just one 'bank' or row of oars on each side. Each oar was about 12 metres long. By the 5th century BC the trireme (above right), rowed by three banks, was the backbone of the Greek fleet.

ROME'S BATTLE FLEETS

Eventually, the city of Rome became the most powerful state in the northern Mediterranean. But when Rome tried to take control of Sicily, she was challenged by the sea-trading empire of Carthage, which the Phoenicians had founded in North Africa. Rome defeated Carthage in a series of sea battles (264-241 BC), using war galleys that were bigger than even the Greek triremes. Roman galleys carried a weighted drawbridge called a 'corvus', or crow (see pages 46-47). This was dropped onto enemy decks so that the Roman soldiers could charge across and capture the ship.

ROMAN MERCHANT SHIPS

By the end of the 1st century BC, Rome's power had spread from one end of the Mediterranean to the other. The Roman Empire depended on trade for its prosperity. Hundreds of merchant ships were constantly at sea. Apart from the tonnes of corn needed to feed all the citizens of the Roman Empire, the ships carried oil and wine in earthenware jars, thousands of wild animals from Asia and Africa, and luxury goods from Asia.

1 **Bow mast**
2 **Mainmast with mainsail brailed (pulled up to yard)**
3 **Cargo hatches**
4 **Stern deckhouse with cabins**
5 **Steering oar**
6 **Grain storage in hold**
7 **Cargo of marble blocks**

SQUARE SAIL AND ARTEMON

We know what Roman merchant ships looked like from pictures on monuments and coins. The hull was deep and rounded. The curving stern-post rose high and was carved into a graceful goose head, which was painted or gilded. The mainmast carried a large square sail, and an angled bow mast carried a smaller sail called an 'artemon'. The ship was steered by twin steering oars linked by a bar which was controlled by a 'helmsman'. The biggest of these ships were at least 50 metres long, and over 13 metres from the deck to the bottom of the hold.

8 **Crossbeams supporting deck**
9 **Cargo of wine in jars (*amphorae*)**
10 **Slaves unloading grain in sacks**
11 **Factory making *amphorae***
12 **Animal escaping from cage**

On this Roman mosaic floor picture, a fisherman is about to cast his anchor so that his boat doesn't drift while he is fishing. The basic shape of the anchor has remained unchanged for hundreds of years.

ACROSS THE PACIFIC

The first human settlers of the islands of the Pacific Ocean - the world's biggest sea - made amazing voyages in their canoes. The Marquesas Islands are at the centre of the map. Also shown is the suggested route of the South American balsa rafts.

Between about 100 BC and 200 AD, while the Roman Empire was at the peak of its power, the first human settlement of the Pacific islands was beginning on the other side of the world.

EAST TO THE MARQUESAS

The first Pacific voyages were made by peoples from mainland Asia. They sailed east in large canoes, seeking new lands in which to live. Finds of their pottery show that as early as 1100 BC they had reached the hundreds of islands between New Guinea and Samoa. By about 300 AD they had reached the Marquesas Islands, over 3,000 kilometres east of Samoa. From there they made further astounding voyages, northwest to Hawaii and southwest to New Zealand.

The fast-sailing 'double canoe' of the Pacific was a type known today as the catamaran. A cross between a simple canoe and a raft, it was built by connecting two canoe-shaped hulls with a central platform.

THE 'DOUBLE CANOE'

The Hawaiian name for the craft that first conquered the Pacific was *wa'a kaulua*, the 'double canoe'. It consisted of two curving hulls joined by a platform, with one or more masts carrying tall sails. These were made of plaited pandanus leaves, and were hooked like crab claws. Europeans exploring the Pacific islands in the 18th century reported that the biggest *wa'a kaulua* were over 30 metres long, and could carry 50 people or more. The *wa'a kaulua* was built of wood, with hollowed tree-trunks forming the undersides of the twin hulls.

Though a fast sailer, the *wa'a kaulua* was light enough to be driven by paddles in calm weather, and was steered by a large paddle at the stern.

Asia · Hawaiian Islands · PACIFIC OCEAN · Balsa rafts · New Guinea · Polynesia · Peru · New Zealand

THE LEGEND OF TIKI

The islanders of southern Polynesia, around Tahiti, trace their beginnings to the god-king Tiki. He is said to have brought the first Polynesians to the islands, sailing not from the west (Asia) but from the east, from 'a big country beyond the sea'. Could they have come from South America?

A South American legend tells of another god-king, Kon-Tiki, or 'Sun-Tiki'. His people had been driven from their great city of Tiahuanaco, in the country we now call Bolivia, around 500 AD. As they fled, Kon-Tiki and the last of his people had reached the Pacific coast and sailed across the sea. Could Kon-Tiki's people have sailed over 7,250 kilometres from South America to Polynesia, using balsa rafts?

ON RAFTS OF BALSA

The peoples who lived in the countries we now call Peru and Bolivia had also become ocean voyagers. Unlike the Pacific islanders, they used rafts instead of canoes. These were made of balsa logs and had square sails. Surely the spongy balsa logs would have become sodden with water, sinking in mid-ocean long before the people reached the South Pacific islands? Or had they really made the voyage?

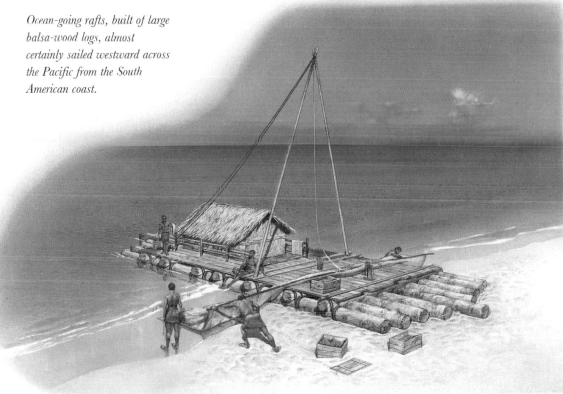

Ocean-going rafts, built of large balsa-wood logs, almost certainly sailed westward across the Pacific from the South American coast.

'When you are on the ocean you cannot see any islands. Only the things we bring with us help us to survive. We act together. That is all I have to say. Remember, all of you, and we will see that place we are going to.'

——— *Mau Piailug, canoe sailing master* ———

TRIUMPH OF THE KON-TIKI

In 1947, Thor Heyerdahl set out to prove they could have done it. He built the *Kon-Tiki*, a balsa-log raft, and sailed it from Peru to Polynesia - 6,920 kilometres in 101 days. There, on a Pacific island, Heyerdahl planted a coconut palm brought from South America, proving that such a voyage could have been made.

RELEARNING TO SAIL

More proof came in 1976 when a replica of an ancient *wa'a kaulua*, named *Hokule'a*, set sail from Hawaii. Navigating using the stars and covering more than 60 kilometres a day, the *Hokule'a* reached Tahiti, 4,800 kilometres to the south. During the 35-day voyage her crew rediscovered some of the sailing skills of the Pacific's first conquerors.

This wooden figure was carved in the Solomon Islands in the 19th century to decorate the prow (front) of a canoe. The figure was the craftsman's way of remembering his ocean-crossing ancestors, and was believed to protect the canoe from evil spirits.

11

SHIPS OF THE VIKINGS

The source of Viking power - a longship on a silver coin made in Denmark and found in Sweden, showing the hull planks and the partly lowered sail.

This busy scene at a Viking port shows knorrs unloading cargo and livestock at the dockside. In the background is a fighting drakkar under sail.

After the fall of the Roman Empire in the 5th century AD, the next advance in European shipbuilding took place in northern waters. This was the construction of tough, seaworthy 'longships'.

THE FIRST LONGSHIPS

The first longships were used by the Angles and Saxons. They rowed rather than sailed these ships, which were open to the sea. One such longship has been discovered in a Danish peat bog. Built of overlapping oak planks, it has positions for 15 oars on each side, and was steered by a paddle-like oar on the right-hand side. This was called the 'steering board', from which comes the word 'starboard', still in use today.

THE VIKING DRAKKARS

However, the real masters of the longship were the Vikings. Between about AD 800 and 1000, the Viking 'drakkars' or 'dragon ships' of Norway, Sweden and Denmark were the terror of Europe. Several have survived, buried in Viking funeral mounds.

Drakkars were designed to be sailed or rowed. When the ship approached land, or when it needed to manoeuvre carefully, the mast and sail were lowered and the crew rowed. The great *Ormr inn langi* or 'Long Serpent', owned by King Olaf Tryggvason of Norway, is said to have had as many as 34 oars a side.

'Bleak showers lashed across
dark prows
Hard along the coast-line;
Iron-shielded vessels
Flaunted colourful rigging.
The great prince saw ahead
The copper roofs of Byzantium;
His swan-breasted ships swept
Towards the tall-towered city.'

— *King Harald's Saga* —

ASHORE AND AFLOAT

Viking ships did not sit deep in the water,
and could be hauled ashore. When they
carried horses or other livestock, the
animals could easily be landed by tipping
the ship over to one side. Although the
planks of the hull were nailed together,
they were tied to the ribs with spruce roots.
This meant the ship was very flexible and
would not be damaged by the pounding
of heavy waves.

When sailing, the Vikings did not have
to rely on following winds. If they wanted
to sail at an angle to the wind, they kept
the sail stretched open with a piece of
wood called a bracing spar, or *beiti ass*.
The bottom timber of the Viking
ship, the keel, helped the ship to
keep a straight course.

CARGO-CARRYING KNORRS

The Vikings were great traders and
colonists, eager to find new markets for
their goods and new lands in which to
settle. But little is known about their cargo
ships, which they called 'knorrs'. The knorr
was developed from the drakkar but was
broader and had higher sides to protect its
stacks of cargo. Knorrs were used to carry
timber to the treeless Norse colonies on
Iceland and Greenland, and to bring back
bales of valuable seal and polar bear fur.

In about 986, a knorr owned by a
merchant seaman named Bjarni sailed
for the new colony of Greenland.
Bjarni was blown far off course by
bad weather, only reaching Greenland
after sighting a strange new land to the
southwest. Later, Leif Eriksson, the son
of Greenland's ruler, bought Bjarni's
knorr and became the first European
to sail down the coast of Labrador
to Newfoundland. Without
knowing it, he had reached
North America over 500 years
before Christopher Columbus.

*These cross-sections of ships, based on
archaeological finds, show how Viking ships
developed. The top two ships do not have a
keel. The third ship has a simple keel and a
wider hull. The fourth vessel, known as the
Oseberg ship, is the first Viking ship known
to have had a mast. The bottom diagram
shows the Gokstad ship, which had a more
substantial keel and a support for the mast.*

*The longship remained the
favourite type of ship in northern
Europe for several hundred
years. This scene from the
Bayeux Tapestry shows
Normans building longship
transports for the invasion of
England in 1066.*

AD 300

AD 400

AD 700

AD 800

AD 850

13

SAILORS OF ARABIA

How the great years of Viking and Arab seafaring overlapped. Throughout the Middle Ages, Arab sailors ruled the seas from Africa to South-East Asia. Although their ships rarely met, the Vikings and Arabs traded together, exchanging goods and slaves.

Chinese

Vikings

Arabs

I n the 7th and 8th centuries AD, the Arabs conquered the Persian Empire, most of the Greek-speaking eastern Roman Empire, the whole coast of North Africa, and Spain. And the Arabs were great sailors as well as outstanding warriors. By 1000 AD, while Greenland's Vikings were voyaging west to North America, Arab navigators were sailing to the East Indies and China.

STITCHING SHIPS TOGETHER

Arab ships could not have been more different to those of the Vikings. The overlapping planks of Viking hulls were stoutly nailed together, while the smooth hulls of Arab ships were built with their planks laid edge to edge. These planks were then stitched together with hundreds of kilometres of cord made from coir, or coconut-fibre. Arab shipbuilders learned that if the coir was regularly soaked with vegetable oil, a ship would last from six to 10 times longer than a ship whose timbers were fastened with iron nails.

Like Egypt, Arabia did not have timber suitable for shipbuilding. So timber was one of the first cargoes brought home by Arab traders. The Egyptians had sailed only 300 kilometres between the Nile and the Lebanon, but the Arabs made voyages of 1,500 kilometres across the Arabian Sea to bring back teak wood from the forests of India.

An Arab boum under full sail, showing the stern rudder and cargo hold beneath the deck. The smell below deck was dreadful, because the ship's planks were swabbed regularly with vegetable oil.

MASTS AND SAILS

The Arabs were great scientists, in every subject from astronomy to medicine. They used these skills in navigation and shipbuilding. They were the first known seafarers to fit their ships with two masts.

Instead of the traditional square sail, the Arabs favoured triangular or 'lateen' sails. The sails were arranged or 'rigged' along the line of the ship's keel, instead of across it. They included a small triangular 'jib' at the ship's bow, which is still used in sailing craft today. The Arabs found that a ship rigged like this could sail closer to the wind (see below), and make progress even when the wind did not blow from astern.

RUDDERS

The Arabs were among the first sailors to fit their ships with rudders for steering. The hinged rudder, hung on stout pins fitted to the ship's stern-post, was much better for controlling a ship's direction than a steering oar. It was one of the most important improvements made to ships during the Middle Ages.

BOUM

The most famous type of ocean-going Arab ship was the boum, 25 metres or more long. The posts at its bow and stern were straight, and it carried large triangular sails on two masts, and a jib. Over 640 kilometres of coir was used on the hull of a boum. The fibre was threaded and knotted through some 20,000 holes, all slowly hand-drilled through the hard teak wood.

lateen sail *mainmast* *jib* *bowsprit* *straight bow-post* *keel* *rudder*

This side view of a typical Arab ship shows the triangular lateen sails, the jib supported by the bowsprit, and the sharp forward 'rake', or slant, of the masts.

RICHES OF THE EAST

Using their great skills and ships like the boum, the Arabs sailed over 4,000 kilometres down the East African coast, and 6,000 kilometres round the coast of India to the East Indies. By the 13th century AD, Arab ships were sailing as far as China, another 2,500 kilometres further north. The wealth of this huge sea-trading empire - silks and spices, jewels and porcelain - remained under Arab control for the next 300 years.

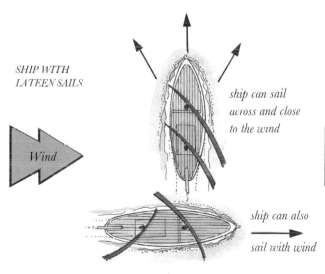

SHIP WITH LATEEN SAILS

ship can sail across and close to the wind

ship can also sail with wind

Wind

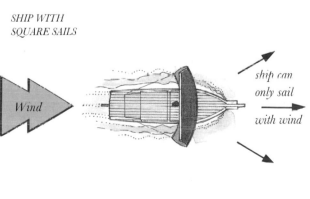

SHIP WITH SQUARE SAILS

Wind

ship can only sail with wind

The sharply-angled posts at the bow and stern stand out in this 13th-century picture of an Arab ship. Notice the efficient looking four-pronged anchor hanging from the bow.

Unlike the square sail (left), which needs winds from astern, fore-and-aft lateen sails (far left) allow a ship to 'reach', or sail across the wind, as well as sail with it.

GIANTS OF THE SEA

The Chinese were skilled navigators. We know that by the 12th century they were using magnetic compasses (above right) to plan their courses.

The Arabs who reached the Far East were the first western people to see the biggest ships in the world. These were the huge trading junks of the Chinese, built to carry passengers as well as cargo.

'We shall tell you first of the ships in which merchants trading with India make their voyages. They are built of spruce and fir. They have one deck; and above this, in most ships, are at least 60 cabins, each of which can comfortably accommodate one merchant.'

Marco Polo

AMAZING SHIPS

The huge Chinese vessels clearly amazed explorer Marco Polo in the 13th century. The big *pechili* junks were 55 metres long and 9 metres across. A junk's hull was made of two thicknesses of planks nailed together and had a flat bottom. Marco also noted that Chinese ships carried only one 'steering oar' - actually a rudder at the stern, another novelty which he had never seen before.

MASTS AND SAILS

Like the Arabs, the Chinese had discovered that ships sail far better with more than one mast. Chinese ships had four masts, and carried two extra ones that could be raised for use when needed. The sails were square, and woven of stout matting instead of cloth. The Chinese stiffened the sails with bamboo slats. These kept the sails stretched, and therefore more efficient at catching even the lightest winds.

WATERTIGHT COMPARTMENTS

Another remarkable feature of China's big junks was their hulls. These were divided into 14 watertight sections by strong walls called bulkheads. If the ship leaked or hit a rock, only one or two sections would be flooded, instead of the whole ship. It was centuries before European ships were designed with bulkheads.

1 **Hull made of two layers of planks**
2 **Watertight bulkheads**
3 **Flat bottom**
4 **Tiller (bar for turning rudder)**
5 **Rudder**
6 **Cargo of baskets of pepper**
7 **Bamboo slats**
8 **Crew's quarters**

This is a large ocean-going junk typical of those seen by Marco Polo when he travelled throughout China around 1275-95. Marco, who had travelled from Venice, one of Europe's most powerful trading nations, wrote in great detail about the ships he saw.

THE EUROPEAN COG

This golden reliquary from 15th century France shows a nef. The nef was a bigger form of the cog, but still had a single mast and sail, plus fore- and sterncastles.

This diagram shows how a cog's winch, called a windlass, could be used for unloading cargo, as well as for raising and lowering the sail and anchor. The yard, from which the sail would hang, is being used like the boom of a crane.

The longship (see page 12) did not vanish with the end of the Viking era in the 11th century. The only real change over the next 150 years was that towers were built at its bow and stern to carry soldiers in time of war - these were called 'forecastles' and 'sterncastles'. But by the middle of the 13th century a new type of ship was emerging: the sturdy cog.

THE HANSEATIC LEAGUE

The years between about 1150 and 1250 saw the growth of wealthy German trading ports like Hamburg, Lübeck, Stralsund and Rostock. To protect and extend their growing trade on the North and Baltic seas, they banded together to form the Hanseatic League. ('Hansa' meant a group or company of allies.) Each of the League's biggest trading cities had its own official seal, which most chose to decorate with a picture of a ship. By the 1240s nearly all these seals (above right) were showing the same type of ship, which is best known as the 'Hansa cog'.

GOODBYE TO THE LONGSHIP

But what was a cog really like? In pictures on seals and in manuscripts, it is clear the cog had a hull of overlapping planks and a single square sail. However, in no other way was it like the old longships. The cog was shorter, broader and deeper. It had straight bow- and stern-posts rising from a straight keel. The hull was not open but had a deck over it. And the biggest change was that the cog had a hinged rudder, not a steering oar. Probably by chance, the Hanseatic shipbuilders had decided to use many features of the Arab boum - which was almost unknown to 13th century German seamen.

THE COG OF BREMEN

Historians argued for many years about the size of cogs, and exactly how they were built. Then, in 1962, a cog was found buried deep in the mud near the old Hanseatic seaport of Bremen. The condition of its timbers showed that this had been a brand-new ship. It had not even been finished when it was swept away in a flood and sunk, probably around 1380.

Built of oak planks, the Bremen cog is 23.5 metres long. Her displacement, or weight in the water, would have been about 138 tonnes. Rising above the main deck she has a sterncastle supporting a heavy winch, called a windlass. This was used to raise and lower the sail and anchor, to hoist cargo in and out of the hold, and also to 'trim' the sail - swinging it to and fro to catch as much wind as possible.

DESIGNED FOR BEACHING

On each side of the Bremen cog, the three lowest planks of the hull were fixed edge to edge, giving the ship a very strong bottom. The cog's straight keel and stout bottom timbers enabled it to be beached. This meant it could deliver goods to places where there were no harbours or docks at which to load and unload. The ship would then float off safely on the next high tide.

yard

sterncastle   windlass

CARGOES OF THE NORTH

Five stout beams run across the Bremen cog from side to side, their ends emerging through the side planking. These beams support the deck, under which lies the deep cargo hold.

Many tough little ships like the Bremen cog carried the goods on which the trade of medieval Europe depended: corn, wine, wool, livestock, timber, iron and pitch. It was in the age of the cog (about 1200-1400) that ships began to be measured by the number of barrels or 'tuns' they could carry as cargo. This is the origin of the word 'tonnage', still used to measure the weight of ships today, and of the modern word 'tonne'.

This 14th-century manuscript shows a battle between cogs, both of which have forecastles and sterncastles. Archers are shooting from the high sterncastle of the ship on the left.

The strong, straight keel and deep rounded hull of a cog was ideal for beaching the ship where there was no convenient harbour for loading and unloading cargo, or for repairing the ship. Props on either side kept the ship upright until the tide floated her off again.

19

OCEAN-CROSSING CARAVELS

Crewmen prepare to set the mainsail of a busy caravel. On deck, the navigator is using a cross-staff to find the ship's position from the height of the sun. This caravel also has an early gun mounted on its rail.

The caravel was small, fast and seaworthy - an ideal ship for making long ocean voyages of discovery. A blend of Mediterranean and north European designs, the caravel made it possible for European adventurers to explore the Atlantic and Indian Oceans.

CLINKER VERSUS CARVEL

In 1400, ships in Europe had been built with overlapping planks, called clinker-building, for over a thousand years. But Mediterranean seamen had found a better way of building ships. In the 15th century this method, called carvel-building, spread to the seafaring countries along Europe's Atlantic coast.

Ships built carvel-style had a smooth hull. The planks were laid edge to edge, over strong frames attached to the keel. This method enabled ships to be built bigger and stronger than clinker-built ones. The smooth plank skin also helped carvel-built ships sail better and faster.

SQUARE SAILS OR LATEEN?

The caravel, which gave its name to 'carvel' building, was a small ship. It was clearly developed from Portuguese ocean-going fishing boats designed for the Atlantic. Pictures of caravels show that they were a mix of old and new. They had a hinged rudder like cogs, but a square stern instead of a pointed one. They had a low rounded bow, and were rigged with two masts and lateen sails like Arab ships. They also carried a third mast in the stern: a mizzenmast.

Cabot and others

Columbus and others

Da Gama and others

Magellan and Del Cano

Some of the ocean routes explored by caravels and other ships between 1450 and 1600, including Magellan and Del Cano's round-the-world voyage.

> **'And because the caravel *Pinta* was swifter and went ahead of the Admiral, it found land and made the signals...At two hours after midnight the land appeared, from which they were two leagues.'**
>
> *Christopher Columbus*

On their long voyages, the sailors of Portugal and Spain discovered that the caravel could be rigged with either lateen or square sails, or better still a combination of both. This mixture of rigs enabled the ship to tack (zig-zag) into the wind, or sail powerfully before a following wind.

REACHING OUT FOR INDIA

Supported by Prince Henry 'The Navigator' (1394-1460), Portuguese caravels began sailing further and further down the unexplored west coast of Africa. By 1460 they were rounding Africa's western 'bulge' and were bringing back cargoes of African gold, ivory and slaves.

Then, in 1488, Bartholomew Diaz sailed even further south, round the Cape of Good Hope and into the Indian Ocean. Ten years later, Vasco da Gama led the first Portuguese trading fleet on the long voyage round Africa to India and back. The caravel had brought the riches of the Indies within the reach of European traders for the first time.

THE FAMOUS *NIÑA*

The most famous caravel was the *Niña*. About 20 metres long and carrying about 60 tonnes of stores and cargo, she was one of three ships used by Christopher Columbus during his first crossing of the Atlantic in 1492. After his flagship *Santa Maria* was wrecked, the great explorer sailed back to Spain in the *Niña*.

The ship's navigator recorded the ship's course using a traverse board (right). Every half an hour, a peg was put in a hole corresponding to the direction the ship was sailing. When he had several recordings, the navigator could then 'plot' or draw the course on a map. He would try to check the position he had calculated by observing the position of the sun and prominent stars.

Above left is a 'caravela latina', with a full lateen rig. Above right is the same ship re-rigged as a 'caravela redonda', with a square mainsail and foresail. Bigger caravels like this sometimes had a small fourth mast astern of the mizzen. This was known as the counter-mizzen, or bonaventure.

This 16th century compass (above left), used for working out the ship's direction, is set in the cover of a book of maps. As well as north, east, south and west, the detailed bearings or 'points' of the compass are shown. The crew measured time using a sandglass like the one above. They knew that the sand took a fixed amount of time to run from the top of the glass, through the narrow neck, to the bottom.

THE STATELY CARRACK

A nocturnal, used by early navigators to measure the time by the position of the stars. Accurate ships' clocks, called chronometers, were not available until the 1770s.

As well as the caravel, the 15th century also produced the large three- and four-masted cargo ship known as the carrack. Carracks were big enough to be armed with cannon for defence, and eventually developed into the first sailing battleships armed with cannon.

STORESHIPS

Although caravels were small and fast, they could only carry small amounts of stores and provisions. Therefore it was usual to send a storeship with them on long voyages of exploration. On the first Atlantic crossing by Columbus in 1492, the caravels *Pinta* and *Niña* were accompanied by the bigger but clumsier storeship *Santa Maria*. Storeships like the *Santa Maria* became common in the 15th century.

By the 1550s, carracks returning to Europe from the Indies carried the richest cargoes afloat. Here the ship on the right has rammed a potentially wealthy victim. It has braved the defender's gunfire to pour a wave of attackers onto the enemy's upper deck.

CARRACKS

Small storeships, like the *Santa Maria*, were described by the Spanish word 'nao', which simply means 'ship'. But in the later 15th century, bigger three-masted storeships were called 'carracks', and they remained in use for over a hundred years.

A little nao like the *Santa Maria* might have as few as 40 crewmen. But big trading carracks like the Spanish *San Felipe* needed twice as many sailors, plus soldiers to defend them. When she was captured sailing home from the East Indies, the *San Felipe's* cargo of spices, silks, gold and jewels was worth more than £1 million in today's money.

TALL CASTLES

Carracks were tall, ungainly ships, with the rounded bow sweeping up to form a towering forecastle, which supported the foremast. Another lofty castle in the stern carried the mizzenmast, and sometimes a counter-mizzen, too.

Carracks usually carried square sails on the fore and mainmasts, and lateen sails on the mizzen and counter-mizzen. A new feature of carracks, such as the Portuguese flagship *Santa Caterina do Monte Sinai*, was the rigging of a small 'topsail' above the mainsail. This gave more pulling power in following winds. The area of sail could also be increased by lacing extra strips, called 'bonnets', to the bottom of the square sails. However, with their high castles and many sails, carracks were also *very* top-heavy.

FOUR DECKS OR MORE

European carracks were maybe only half as long as the big Chinese junks, which had only one deck. But the carracks were taller ships, with at least four decks for cargo stowage, passenger accommodation and crew living quarters. Some carracks had as many as six decks, with the extra decks in the high castles.

The deck and mast layout of a big 16th-century carrack. From the bottom, the decks were called the orlop or lower deck (below the waterline); the main deck; and the quarterdeck (astern of the mainmast). There was a short poopdeck above the quarterdeck in the stern, and the tall forecastle usually contained two short decks.

In this painting of about 1520, ships fill Antwerp harbour, one of the leading ports of the 16th century. In the centre is a large four masted carrack with square and lateen sails. A topsail can be seen at the top of its mainmast. To defend their cargoes, carracks carried a wide range of light guns in their castles and upper decks. To the left of the carrack is a galley, widely used by Spain, Venice and Portugal.

CAGES AND GUNPORTS

Pictures of early 16th century carracks show the upper decks covered with what look like untiled roofs. These 'cages' were in fact a defence against enemies trying to get on board, and they could be covered with netting to make boarding even harder. Another feature added to carracks were rows of holes, or gunports, cut through the sides of the castles, through which light cannon could be fired. Later, when carracks were built with ports for heavy guns on the maindeck, a new age of naval warfare began.

Transporting horses and other livestock by sea was a problem. Rough weather would make them fall and break their legs. This is one of the ways used to secure the animals below decks.

counter-mizzen mizzenmast mainmast foremast

poop deck forecastle bowsprit
quarterdeck

cage

main deck

orlop deck

ARMADA GALLEONS

Above is an early naval gun, recovered from the English Mary Rose, sunk in 1545. Its barrel was an iron sheet bent into a tube, strengthened with iron hoops. By the time of the Armada, most big guns were cast in one piece from bronze or iron (right). The powder, charge and shot were rammed down the barrel through the muzzle.

The increased use of cannons in the 16th century marked the end of a style of naval warfare which originated in the sea battles of Ramesses III in ancient Egypt. Now warships carried powerful guns as well as soldiers who could storm and capture other ships. These guns could even win a sea battle without soldiers becoming directly involved.

A one-piece gun, about 2.5 metres long, being recovered from the Spanish Armada ship El Gran Grifon.

THE FIRST BROADSIDES

At first, guns were used to batter the decks of approaching enemy ships. They shot at the enemy troops to make it easier for their own soldiers to board and capture the enemy ship. But it was still the soldiers' bows and arrows, spears and swords that won battles. The rows of guns, firing through ports cut in the sides of the ship, became known as 'broadsides'.

GALLEYS AND GALLEASSES

Guns were also useful additions to the oldest of all warship types, the oared galley. By the 1540s the use of guns mounted in broadsides, combined with oars for rowing in calm Mediterranean weather, had produced a new type of warship. This was the galleass (top): a galley with three masts, and a broadside of light guns above the rowing deck.

An impatient captain looks on as one of his crew receives treatment from the ship's 'barber surgeon'. Only the biggest warships carried a barber surgeon for treating sickness and wounds, and their 'expert treatment' was fairly primitive. The large sailcloth bundle contains the body of a dead crewman, sewed up ready for burial at sea.

GALLEYS AT LEPANTO

The last great battle between fleets of oared warships took place off Greece, at Lepanto, in 1571. A fleet of 208 galleasses and galleys from Spain, Malta and Venice destroyed a Turkish fleet of 273 galleys. Lepanto seemed to prove that cannon-armed galleys and galleasses were valuable fighting ships - and so they were, against ships of their own type. But the Spanish Armada battles, described below, showed that galleasses could not hope to defeat agile sailing ships armed with broadsides, especially in the rougher conditions of the Atlantic.

'GREAT SHIPS' AND GALLEONS

At the time of Lepanto, huge sailing ships of 1,000 tonnes were being built. But the newest type of sailing warship was the smaller, slimmer 'galleon', faster and more agile than these 'great ships'. To galleon designers, it was better to use the decks for cannon than to pack them with soldiers. The most famous English galleon, *Revenge*, displaced 447 tonnes and carried 34 guns. In contrast, Spain's 1,000-tonne *San Martin* was crammed with 300 soldiers but carried only 14 more cannon than the *Revenge*.

In 1588, Spain sent a great 'Armada' to escort its army across the English Channel. This resulted in the first battle between fleets of galleons armed with broadsides. The English captains did not try to board the Spanish ships. Instead, they relied on gunfire, swiftly turning their faster galleons to fire one broadside after another. This enabled them to fire twice the weight of shot at the bigger but slower enemy ships.

"The Spanish fleet edged up to succour (aid) their galleasses, and so rescued them and the galleon, after which time they were never seen in fight any more, so badly was their entertainment in this encounter.'

--- *Lord Howard of Effingham* ---

In the Armada campaign, the English and Spanish fleets had about the same number of ships. But, in four battles, Spain's galleons, great ships and galleasses never once came to grips with the English fleet, and the invasion was abandoned.

In this painting of an Armada battle, we can see how ships swarmed around their enemies like angry bees. However, the artist has made little distinction between England's low and slim galleons (red crosses on white flags) and Spain's larger ships (yellow crosses on red). In the foreground is a galleass

Even though the galley (kitchen) fire was enclosed by bricks to prevent sparks burning the ship, it was only safe to cook hot food when the weather was calm.

EAST INDIAMEN

This is not an outsize pocket watch, but John Harrison's Chronometer No 4. This was the first timepiece able to keep running on voyages round the world, making navigation much more accurate.

This fine picture shows East Indiamen of the Dutch East India Company. The artist has captured every detail beautifully.

Because of the discoveries of its sea captains, Portugal had taken control of the rich sea trade with India and the Far East. However, by 1600 the European sea powers were battling to seize the biggest share of this trade. For the next 250 years, large, well-armed merchant ships known to all seamen as 'East Indiamen' carried precious cargoes from the Orient.

THE EAST INDIA COMPANIES

The 17th century saw the founding of the famous 'East India Companies' - the English in 1600, the Dutch in 1602, the Danish in 1616 and the French in 1664. The merchants who ran the companies had one goal above all: to make profits and wealth through trade. The companies hired their own sailors, soldiers and well-armed ships to bring home the cargoes - and to fight if necessary.

FOR PEACE OR WAR

The profits from a successful East India voyage ran into millions (the captain of an East Indiaman would earn at least £5,000 per voyage), but the risks and dangers were also high. To overcome them, a new type of ship was built.

The handsome East Indiamen of the 17th and 18th centuries (above) were really a cross between the heavy trading carracks and the swift fighting galleons of the 16th century. Although they had fewer guns than a warship of the same size, the early ones could carry about 350 tonnes of cargo. By the late 18th century, European East Indiamen were the finest ships afloat, and their decks could hold over 1,000 tonnes. They had to be able to carry a very wide range of goods, on both outward and homeward voyages. A typical outward-bound cargo would include gold and silver, iron, lead and copper, cloth and finished clothes, household goods, building bricks, tiles and drink - barrels of beer, wine, gin and brandy.

PERILS OF THE VOYAGE

The East Indiamen also carried important passengers to and from the Indies. These people demanded comfortable quarters, so the ships were fitted with luxury cabins.

The 16,000-kilometre voyage round Africa to India took four months, and that to China nearly six. The sailors had to be ready at all times to fight off rivals and pirates. Quite apart from the risks of shipwreck and casualties in battle, a crew could easily lose a man every 10 days from accidents or disease. So East Indiamen sailed with as many as 250 crew and passengers to allow for these losses.

An East Indiaman in a breaming dock (right). Here the massive growths of seaweed and barnacles that built up on a long ocean voyage were burned off. The ship's underside was then scraped clean and the seams between the planks were made waterproof with tar in preparation for the next voyage.

THE LOSS OF THE 'WHITE LION'

A typical sea battle resulted in the sinking of the 30-gun Dutch East Indiaman *Witte Leeuw* ('White Lion') in 1613. Sailing with three other ships, she was returning from the Indies with a priceless cargo: 1,311 diamonds, a hold full of delicate Chinese porcelain ware and over 15,000 bags of pepper, as well as other costly spices. At St Helena in the South Atlantic, the Dutch ships found two rival Portuguese ships which they immediately attacked! But the Portuguese fought back. Their gunfire started a blaze which exploded *Witte Leeuw's* gunpowder and sank her and her entire cargo.

The later East Indiamen were so powerfully armed, with broadsides of 50 guns or more, that they were used as warships in times of war. In February 1804, a convoy of East Indiamen chased away an enemy battle fleet off the coast of Malaya. The battle fleet's admiral retreated because he thought the well-armed East Indiamen were heavy ships of war.

'All at Sea', a cartoon showing after-dinner chaos aboard a storm-tossed East Indiaman. Even the wealthiest passengers in their luxury cabins could not escape from the miseries of rough weather.

Beautiful Chinese porcelain ware, part of a rich cargo recovered by divers from the wreck of a 17th century East Indiaman.

SHITS OF THE LINE

The gun decks of a First Rate, showing the inward slope or 'tumble-home' of the sides. The gunpowder was stored safely below the waterline in a 'magazine'.

After the defeat of the Spanish Armada, warship designers strove to increase the fire-power of the fighting galleon. The result was the heavy sailing warship known as the 'ship of the line', with three decks and 100 guns or more.

THREE-DECKED GIANTS

The 1580s galleon carried its guns on the main and quarterdecks. It seemed easy enough to design bigger ships armed with two full decks of guns instead of one. Unfortunately, many of the first 'two-deckers' were too narrow and top-heavy. Several capsized, such as the 1,300-tonne Swedish *Vasa* which turned over in harbour on her maiden voyage in 1628.

The answer to top-heaviness in big ships was to have a hull with a pear-shaped cross-section, with the upper hull sides sloping inwards. The heaviest guns were mounted on the lowest deck for stability. This system produced warships which were the biggest and most powerful ships for the next 250 years.

GUNS AND CREW

At this time, guns were named by the weight of shot they fired. A typical 'three-decker' would carry 32-pounder guns on the lower gun deck, 24-pounders on the middle deck and 12-pounders on the upper deck. Other guns were mounted on the quarterdeck and forecastle.

An 80-gun 'three-decker' like France's *Bucentaure* would have a crew of about 800 officers and men. On board these ships, conditions were hard. Men had a space less than 60 centimetres wide in which to sling their hammocks (canvas beds hung up at the end by cords), and, with fresh food unavailable on long voyages, disease could be as big a danger as enemy shot.

Action on the upper deck. The gun crew have just reloaded, and have run out the gun using ropes and pulleys. They are now aiming it for the next broadside. To the left, a soldier is firing his musket at troops in an enemy ship's rigging.

THE LINE OF BATTLE

By the late 17th century, ships no longer fought individual battles at sea. Instead, admirals used their broadsides by sailing their ships in a formation known as the 'line of battle'. The lines of ships would sail past each other less than 500 metres apart, their guns pounding the enemy.

Only the most powerful warships were considered fit for the line of battle. These, the battleships of the age of sail, became known as 'ships of the line'. They were graded or 'rated' by the number of guns they carried. First Rates had 100 guns or more, Second Rates 84-100, Third Rates 70-84, and Fourth Rates 50-70 guns. By the 1790s, Fifth Rates (32-50 guns) were no longer considered fit for the line of battle.

THE MIGHTY *SANTISSIMA*

During the 1760s, France began to strengthen its navy. As well as building fast and powerful ships, the French navy paid special attention to improving its gunnery. Moreover, France and Spain built bigger First Rates than their greatest rival, Britain, and armed them with heavier guns (36- and 48-pounders). The biggest First Rate of all was Spain's four-decked *Santissima Trinidad* with 136 guns. Like many First Rate ships of the line, the *Santissima* had a thick oak hull that could withstand all but the heaviest broadside.

Britain's response to powerful ships like the *Santissima* was to train its gun crews brutally until they could fire at least three broadsides to the enemy's two. The ships would try to cut across the enemy's bow or stern and 'rake' him - firing broadsides that smashed from one end of the ship to the other. Just one 'raking' broadside could inflict fearful damage. This was the fate of the *Santissima Trinidad* in the Battle of Trafalgar in 1805. The 98-gun British *Neptune* got under *Santissima*'s stern and raked her repeatedly until she surrendered. The *Santissima* was so badly damaged that she later sank.

Although they were built for war, some ships of the line were beautifully decorated. In this Dutch painting of a battle in 1666, the gilded carving, called 'gingerbread', can be seen on the stern and hull sides. One tactic was to fire down the length of the ship through the less protected bow or stern.

solid roundshot

chain-shot

bar-shot

A loaded gun. The shot was kept from rolling out of the gun by being sandwiched in place between felt pads known as wads. Whirling through the air like scythes, chain-shot and bar-shot were used to disable enemy ships by slicing their rigging to pieces.

A beautiful and detailed model of a Second Rate ship of the line from the 17th century. This is the Dutch Friesland, *which fought in the Battle of Solebay in 1672.*

The large passenger-carrying steamships had much better facilities than the wooden sailing ships that preceded them. This is a glazed toilet from the Great Britain, *a luxury unknown on early warships.*

Ten years after Trafalgar, the world's first working ships powered by steam engines were in service. These were small tugboats driven by paddle-wheels. Over the next 30 years, the first ocean crossings were made using steam power, and the first ships were built with iron frames and plating instead of wood.

STEAM GOES AFLOAT

The first steam-powered ships to be of practical use were the 17-metre, single-paddle tugboat *Charlotte Dundas* in Scotland, built in 1802, and the larger, twin-paddle *Clermont* in America, in 1807. The *Clermont*, pictured above right, was the first steamboat to carry passengers. However, it was 40 years before steam engines were able to provide the main power for ocean-going ships. Even then, steamships were given a full rig of sails in case the machinery broke down.

FULL STEAM AHEAD

By the 1840s, steam-powered ships were advanced enough to ensure that freight deliveries and passengers arrived on time, whatever the wind and weather. At the same time, industry was now able to forge heavy girders, cast machine parts and roll strong plates. This meant that ships could be made completely of iron, and so could be built much bigger and stronger than was possible with wood. And with an iron hull there was less risk of fires caused by the engine furnaces and funnel sparks. For shipowners, bigger ships meant larger cargoes, more passengers and bigger profits.

A day of glory: Great Britain *is towed down-river to begin her first transatlantic crossing in 1845, which she made in just under 15 days. During her three-week stay in New York, she earned her owners an extra $250 each day, as 1,000 admiring visitors paid 25 cents each to tour the ship.*

BRUNEL'S *GREAT BRITAIN*

These great advances in shipbuilding are typified by the *Great Britain*, designed in 1845 by Isambard Kingdom Brunel. No ship has ever been built with more new developments in design and technology.

With a length of 98 metres and weighing over 3,600 tonnes, the *Great Britain* was the first big iron ship ever built. She was the first ocean-going steamship to rely on a stern propeller instead of big side paddlewheels. This propeller had six blades and measured 4.9 metres across - bigger than any propeller built before. On her trials, the *Great Britain*'s engines drove her at 11 knots (about 18 kilometres per hour).

Brunel also designed a streamlined, balanced rudder (instead of using the traditional rudder like a hinged plate), to make the ship easier to steer. This new type of rudder, and the six-bladed propeller, are still used on ships today.

ALL FOR PASSENGER COMFORT

The *Great Britain* was designed to make fast and comfortable Atlantic crossings. She was fitted with special keels to make her roll less in rough weather. This made travelling more comfortable for the passengers. The ship had 26 single and 113 double passenger cabins, and her hull had several watertight bulkheads. She was the biggest, safest passenger-carrying ship since the giant Chinese junks of over 500 years earlier. The *Great Britain* served from 1845 to 1886, when she was abandoned in the Falkland Islands.

Passengers admire the spacious interior of the Great Britain. *She was the first ship designed and built specifically as a luxury liner.*

Some of the more unusual designs for ships' propellers, which are known as screws.

SUBMARINE ATTACK!

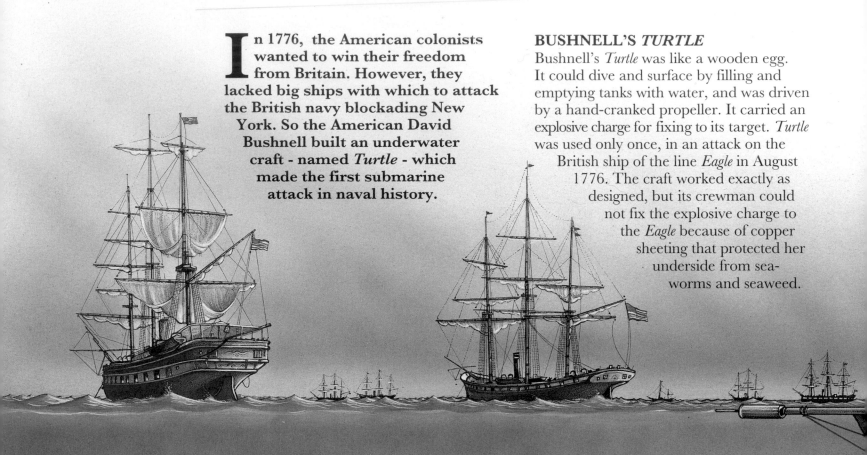

In 1776, the American colonists wanted to win their freedom from Britain. However, they lacked big ships with which to attack the British navy blockading New York. So the American David Bushnell built an underwater craft - named *Turtle* - which made the first submarine attack in naval history.

BUSHNELL'S *TURTLE*

Bushnell's *Turtle* was like a wooden egg. It could dive and surface by filling and emptying tanks with water, and was driven by a hand-cranked propeller. It carried an explosive charge for fixing to its target. *Turtle* was used only once, in an attack on the British ship of the line *Eagle* in August 1776. The craft worked exactly as designed, but its crewman could not fix the explosive charge to the *Eagle* because of copper sheeting that protected her underside from sea-worms and seaweed.

BUSHNELL'S *TURTLE*

1 Water ballast tank
2 Propeller
3 Screw for attaching charge to underside of ship
4 Explosive charge attached to screw
5 Breathing tube
6 Steering gear

THE SOUTHERN 'DAVIDS'

When the American Civil War broke out in 1861, the Confederate states of the South used craft called 'Davids' to fight the powerful fleet of the northern Union states. These cigar-shaped craft could submerge just below the surface. They were armed with a 'spar torpedo', an explosive charge held out on a long pole. Some 'Davids' (above left) had a small steam engine, but most were powered by an eight-man crew turning a long shaft.

The 'Davids' were submersibles. They could not dive deeply, but were weighted to run just below the surface, in calm water only - a rough sea would flood and sink them. The eight human pistons of the 'David' H. L. Hunley, sweating at their long crankshaft in increasingly bad air, had to crouch with their backs against the submersible's curved sides.

THE 'DAVIDS' ATTACK

The original David, so-named because it seemed like a tiny David attacking the enemy's huge Goliath, was steam-powered, with a crew of three. On the night of 5 October 1863 she steamed out to attack New Ironsides, the most powerful ship in the Union fleet. When the David's torpedo exploded on New Ironsides' waterline, the Union ship was saved only by her armour plating.

The second 'David' attack was made by the man-powered H.L. Hunley on the night of 17 February 1864. A small raised hatch enabled the commander to see where he was going. Hunley's torpedo blew a huge hole in the Union's wooden warship Housatonic - the first ship ever sunk by a submarine. But the explosion also swamped and sank the Hunley, drowning all her brave crew.

The Confederate submersible H. L. Hunley *makes its attack on the* Housatonic, *its spar torpedo pointing forward. Turn over the see-through page below to see inside the* Hunley. *The air is getting hotter and sweatier as the crew work to drive it through the water. The box on the opposite page shows David Bushnell's* Turtle. *Both the* Hunley *and the* Turtle *made their attacks at night, moving just below the surface.*

1 Spar torpedo
2 'Diving plane' helping to keep
   craft just below surface
3 Wheel for steering
4 Commander
5 Pump and ballast tank
6 Crankshaft
7 Rudder

THE NEW IRONCLADS

By the 1850s, wooden warships were facing a new threat: guns firing explosive shells instead of solid shot. Against the bursting power of these shells, ships had only one protection - armour plating. The age of a new breed of warship, the steam-driven 'ironclad', had begun.

Combat de Cienfuegos (Cuba)
Une batterie du navire américain 'Marblehead' pendant l'action.

BELTS OF ARMOUR

The world's first ironclads were the French *Gloire* and the British *Warrior*. The *Gloire* (above right), launched in 1859, was the first warship to be given special protection from shellfire. She was a wooden steam frigate with a 'belt' of armoured plates around her waterline to protect her engine-room and guns. The *Warrior*, launched in 1860, was the first steam warship built completely of iron. The *Warrior* was given additional protection by armour plates 11 cm thick, backed by 45 cm of very hard teak wood.

This cross-section of an early ironclad shows the engines located below the waterline, the uptake for a funnel at the centre, and a belt of armour (iron plate backed by teak) protecting the centre of the ship above the waterline.

A sweating gun crew, stripped to the waist, work in the turret of the American ironclad Marblehead *during the Spanish-American War of 1898. The curved rail used for 'training' the gun from side to side can be seen.*

IRONCLADS IN BATTLE

Ironclads proved their resilience under fire during the American Civil War. The Confederates, facing the much larger Union navy, salvaged an abandoned wooden steam-powered frigate, the *Merrimack*, and armed and plated her hull. In March 1862, in her first battle, she sank one frigate by ramming and caused another to run aground.

The next day the *Merrimack* was challenged by the Unionist *Monitor*. The *Merrimack* had 10 guns to *Monitor's* two, but *Monitor's* guns were mounted in a rotating turret, not in fixed broadsides. The two ironclads battered each other at point-blank range for nearly three hours, but neither could seriously damage the other.

SINKING BY RAMMING

As well as proving that armour protected ships, the *Merrimack* seemed to teach another lesson. This was that a steam-powered ironclad could use one of the oldest tactics in naval warfare: ramming enemy ships to sink them. From then on, all new ironclads were given a pointed and armoured bow for ramming. In fact, very few ships were ever sunk by ramming.

THE TURRET-RAM *BUFFEL*

By 1868, ships like the *Buffel* ('Buffalo'), built for the Dutch Navy, were being produced. The Dutch wanted their new warship to have all the important features proved in battle since 1862 - armoured protection, guns mounted in a turret instead of in fixed broadsides, and an armoured bow for ramming. With neither gun-decks nor sails, *Buffel* looked nothing like the first ironclads launched only eight years before.

ATTACK AND DEFENCE

Apart from the menacing curve of her armoured ram, jutting forward below the waterline, *Buffel's* 'teeth' were her two stubby guns firing explosive shells 23 cm in diameter. They were mounted in a low circular turret protected by 20 cm of armour plate backed by 30 cm of teak. *Buffel's* armoured belt was strongest where it protected the boilers and engines near the centre of the ship - 15 cm thick backed by 25 cm of teak. It extended a full metre above and below the waterline. *Buffel* was one of the first ships to have twin screw propellers, her engines providing a top speed of just under 13 knots. She had a crew of 102 officers and men. Splendidly restored, she can still be seen in Rotterdam.

The first battle between ironclads took place in March 1862. The tiny Monitor *(in the foreground) was described by one spectator as looking 'like a tin can on a plank'.*

Built only six years after the Merrimack *and* Monitor, *the Dutch ironclad* Buffel *had a central turret armed with two heavy guns.*

THE CLIPPER YEARS

Some of the main clipper routes and cargoes - emigrants to California, tea from China, and wool from Australia.

*California clippers
1840s-1850s* →

*China tea clippers
1860s-1870s* →

*Australia wool clippers
1870s-1890s* →

The sailing ships of the 19th century had beautiful figureheads, such as this lady cloaked in the American flag.

The famous clippers were the fastest and the most beautiful sailing ships ever built. For the clippers, whose great years lasted from the 1840s to the 1880s, only one thing mattered - speed.

BUILT FOR SPEED

To compete with steamships, clippers were built to make fast long-distance voyages. They specialised in carrying passengers and cargoes that would perish on longer journeys. Instead of the sturdy rounded hull of a typical East Indiaman, the clippers had a sharp, blade-like hull. This was designed to slice through heavy seas under as many sails as their captains dared set - no matter how strong the wind or foul the weather. With 2,900 square metres of canvas and driven at speeds up to 17 knots, clippers were the fastest ships ever to rely on sail alone.

THE CALIFORNIA CLIPPERS

The first and fastest clippers were American-built ships that carried emigrants seeking gold to the goldfields in California (1848) and Australia (1850). The distance from New York to California (round Cape Horn) was about the same as that from London to Melbourne, 30,570 kilometres, and the fastest clippers of the 1850s covered the distance in 65 days.

Journey's end, and the first clippers home unload the highly-prized pick of the Chinese tea crop.

NO LIFE FOR WEAKLINGS

In contrast, the tea clippers did not carry passengers. Their cargoes of tea from China were sealed to keep out the seas which frequently swept the decks. In a hard-driven clipper, the crew (only 30 or less of the toughest seamen of all time) often went without hot food for days, because it was too rough to light the galley fire. In such conditions, a man lost overboard stood little chance of surviving.

THE GREAT CLIPPER RACES

By the mid-19th century, clippers from many countries were carrying passengers and mining equipment to California and Australia. However, in the late 1860s, every clipper owner dreamed of winning the prestigious race to bring the first tea cargo of each year from China to London.

In 1866 the most dramatic of the tea clipper races took place, between *Ariel*, *Taeping* and *Serica*. All three sailed from the great China tea port of Foochow within minutes of each other on 30 May. After 99 days of all-out racing over 33,000 kilometres, *Taeping* docked at London at 9.45 pm on 6 September, followed by *Ariel* at 10.15, and *Serica* at 11.45!

TRADE WITH AUSTRALIA

Even these splendid voyages could not win back the world's ocean trade from steam. The days of the China clippers were ended by the opening of the Suez Canal in 1869. This enabled the coal-hungry steamships to take a shorter route through the Mediterranean Sea, instead of around Africa. Previously, they had been forced to make several expensive stops to refuel.

Some large clippers were able to survive by trading with South America and Australia, partly because there were too few coaling stations on the route. In the 1880s, ships such as the *Cutty Sark* were able to bring wool from Australia to London in around 67 days. But even huge ships like Germany's 5,000-tonne, five-masted *Preussen*, launched in 1902, could not halt the steamship's plodding and irresistible progress.

The splendid clouds of canvas gracing clippers under full sail were favourite subjects with artists. This is the American Sovereign of the Seas, a giant of over 2,400 tonnes. She set an all time sailing record of 13 days 14 hours from New York to Liverpool, at times reaching the incredible speed (for a sailing ship) of 22 knots.

Aboard an American emigrant clipper, a passenger has broken the rules and tried to climb the rigging. He has been caught and tied there by crewmen, and not released until he has bought his freedom with a bottle of rum!

DREADNOUGHTS

Early in the 20th century, the most powerful warships were the Dreadnoughts. Encased in steel armour, and armed with turret-mounted heavy guns with a range of 25 kilometres or more, the Dreadnoughts were the costliest and most destructive weapon that the world had ever seen.

THE TORPEDO THREAT

From the 1870s, new weapons and new inventions forced dramatic changes in warship design. Sails and masts vanished at last, as engines improved and more coal could be carried. There was also a deadly new naval weapon, the self-propelled torpedo, which ran underwater before exploding against the hull of the ship. Designers now had to install more guns in turrets so they could be aimed at fast-moving torpedo-firing ships (above right).

A COMBINATION OF GUNS

By 1900, battleships no longer carried the largest possible number of heavy guns, as in the days of sail. Instead they were also armed with light guns. These were easier to aim at small, fast torpedo-boats that would try to fire their torpedoes at close range. In 1905, a typical battleship was armed with 12 or more light 'quick-firers', ten 6-inch guns, and four 9.25-inch guns. It carried only four of the heaviest 12-inch guns, two forward and two aft.

Britain's Dreadnought *at sea in 1906. The slanting booms along her sides could be swung out to support heavy nets, designed to protect the ship from torpedo attack.*

FISHER'S *DREADNOUGHT*

Most of these guns did not have the range or the power to sink the enemy's biggest ships. When Admiral Fisher became chief of the British navy in 1904, he ordered the building of a new type of battleship. The *Dreadnought* was completed in 1906 after only 14 months. She was the first 'all big-gun' battleship. Her ten 12-inch guns could fire twice as many heavy shells as any other ship afloat, to a range of over 15,000 metres. Compare that with ships of the line of the early 19th century, which fought less than 500 metres apart!

The *Dreadnought* was powered by new steam turbine engines driving four screws. This enabled her to steam at over 20 knots. The *Dreadnought* was also heavily protected, with an armour belt 28 cm thick. In total she displaced over 18,000 tonnes, over 20 times more than most Armada galleons.

A section through a big-gun turret, showing the armoured drum or barbette on which the turret rested. Also visible are the hoists that raised shells and their cordite charges from the shell-room and magazine to the gun crew in the turret.

NEW BUILDING

The *Dreadnought* gave Britain an important technological lead over her most powerful naval rival, Germany. However, this meant that all her older battleships had to be replaced. Now countries such as Germany, France, Japan and the USA had a chance to build large fleets of modern Dreadnoughts to rival Britain's.

By the time World War 1 broke out in August 1914, new 'super-Dreadnoughts' were being built. These weighed as much as 33,500 tonnes and carried eight 15-inch guns. By using oil fuel, which burned more cleanly and was much easier to store than coal, these new Dreadnoughts could reach a speed of 25 knots.

THE BATTLE OF JUTLAND

The only battle between the British and German Dreadnought fleets took place off Jutland, Denmark, on 31 May 1916. It was the biggest battleship fight of the 20th century, with 16 German Dreadnoughts ranged against 28 British. Both fleets, fearing torpedo attacks, stayed at long range. The British fleet lost more ships than the German fleet, but the latter returned to port and never again risked a major battle. Although battleships saw action in World War 2, control of the sea had passed to aircraft carriers and submarines.

In the 1980s, the United States Navy took two of its old battleships from storage and gave them a new lease of life by equipping them with cruise missiles. Cruise missiles can hit a target hundreds of kilometres away with great accuracy. The battleships kept their huge 16-inch guns, which are being fired in this dramatic picture. They are unlikely ever to be fired at enemy ships, but have been used to bombard targets on land.

QUEEN OF THE ATLANTIC

The main picture shows the Normandie. *Renowned for her spacious design, the liner's interior was decorated by some of France's finest artists. The panel below is typical of the many striking scenes on the ship. You can turn over the see-through page to look inside the* Normandie, *and into one of her twin-berth staterooms.* Normandie's *passenger facilities were the most luxurious afloat. Equipped to outclass the world's finest hotels, all First Class rooms included a telephone and a private bath or shower.*

By 1900 the passenger shipping lines of Europe and America were competing to provide the fastest, most luxurious passenger service across the North Atlantic. The race was on for the 'Blue Riband of the Atlantic', awarded to the liner making the quickest crossing.

THE LOVELY *NORMANDIE*

France's *Normandie* was designed to be the biggest, fastest and most beautiful liner in the world. When she entered service in May 1935, the *Normandie* caused a sensation. She was awe-inspiring. From a high flaring bow - designed to prevent waves breaking over the deck - her beautiful lines swept gracefully aft to an elegantly curved stern.

BUILT FOR LUXURY

The *Normandie* was built to provide 1,975 passengers with the ultimate in high-speed luxury and elegance while crossing the Atlantic. As well as over 300 crew, there were nearly 1,000 domestic staff to provide services as good as any hotel on shore.

The *Normandie* had the most modern engines available. Steam from her oil-fired boilers drove four electric motors, each one connected to a separate propeller shaft. Using about 5,000 tonnes of oil per transatlantic crossing, *Normandie* could steam at up to 32 knots.

1 **First Class staterooms and cabins**
2 **Tourist Class accommodation**
3 **First Class Dining Saloon**
4 **Grand Salon (First Class lounge)**
5 **Theatre (with children's playroom above, under funnel)**
6 **Chapel**
7 **Swimming pool**
8 **Crew's quarters**

SPACE AND BEAUTY

The *Normandie* was also remarkable for her huge areas of open deck space, giving an unbroken sweep of 152 metres of public rooms inside. Her mighty hull held 13 levels, from the Upper Sun Deck to 'H' Deck far below the waterline. The superb First Class Dining Saloon was longer than the famous 'Hall of Mirrors' in France's Palace of Versailles, and there was even a separate dining saloon for passengers' servants. The finest artists and decorators made the *Normandie* a showcase of French art in the 1930s, with an attention to detail seen in no other ship. The *Normandie* was famed for her beautiful coloured glass, used for wall decoration as well as lighting.

The *Normandie* fulfilled all hopes by winning the Blue Riband on her maiden voyage with a speed of 29.98 knots. Sadly, while marooned in New York by the out-break of World War 2, she was destroyed by fire and sunk in 1942.

Always the show-piece of the luxury liner, the First Class Dining Saloon (left) broke all previous records in size, beauty and grandeur. During the afternoon, First Class passengers could take refreshments and dance in the Grand Salon (below), where grand balls and concerts were held after dinner. Children were entertained in the children's theatre and playroom (bottom). Children crossing in the Normandie were not only assured of a wonderful time, but the care given to their non-stop entertainment made it possible for their parents to enjoy themselves to the full!

9 **Garage on 'G' Deck**
10 **Ship's stores**
11 **Cargo hold on 'H' Deck**
12 **Boilers**
13 **Electric motors (turbines)**
14 **Kitchens**

THE DEADLY U-BOATS

The special 'Submarine War Badge', awarded only to the U-boat crewmen of the German Navy (Kriegsmarine).

A section through a German Type VII U-boat. Astern of the central control room are the diesel engines used on the surface, and the electric motors used when running submerged. A torpedo has just been fired, and the Captain has turned his periscope to look for another target.

In both World Wars, the torpedo-firing submarine was found to be a deadly weapon against every form of surface ship. Victory or defeat could depend on the ability of ships to survive against fleets of enemy submarines.

THE DEADLY U-BOAT

In 1898 an American inventor, John Holland, built the first practical submarine. But it was the German U-boat - from the German word *unterseeboot* or 'undersea boat' - that proved the submarine could be an effective weapon. From the outbreak of World War 1 in 1914, U-boats threatened the much bigger battleship fleets of Britain and France. But the German High Command also used U-boats to sink over *10 million tonnes* of merchant shipping on which its enemy's war effort depended. The most successful U-boat of all, *U-35*, sank an amazing 224 merchant ships between 1914 and 1918.

By the spring of 1917, victory for the U-boats seemed in sight, but the Allies found the answer just in time. By sailing the merchant ships in groups called convoys, protected by an escort of warships, they greatly reduced their losses.

These are the cramped conditions in which crews lived and worked. They stood no chance if the U-boat's watertight hull was cracked by depth charges. Until the invention of nuclear power, submarines had to surface often to re-charge their electric batteries using their air-breathing diesel engines.

THE TYPE VII U-BOAT

During World War 2, the Allies again faced the U-boat threat. The main U-boat used by the German navy was called the Type VII. A typical Type VII U-boat was 67 metres long, displaced 781 tonnes on the surface but 885 tonnes when submerged with its tanks flooded.

The Type VII's deadly armament was its 14 torpedoes, each of which could sink a large merchant ship. The torpedoes could be fired from four torpedo tubes in the bow and another one in the stern. A typical Type VII also carried a powerful 8.8 cm gun and three light anti-aircraft guns in case it had to fight on the surface.

A DANGEROUS LIFE

Life for a U-boat's 44 officers and men was extremely uncomfortable and hazardous. When close to their enemy, they often had to remain submerged for hours on end. There was often a shortage of oxygen, as poisonous fumes from the U-boat's diesel engines built up in the cramped quarters.

In addition, by 1939 the British and French had found a way of detecting a submerged U-boat. This was by using sonar (SOund Navigation And Ranging). Sonar sent out a sound pulse which returned an echo or 'ping' on hitting the hull of any nearby U-boat. The U-boat hunter would then try to sail over the U-boat and drop 'depth-charges'. These were bombs set to explode at the U-boat's estimated depth.

BATTLE OF THE ATLANTIC

Even with these and other electronic devices for hunting U-boats, Britain and later the USA came very close to defeat in the 'Battle of the Atlantic' (1940-1943). 'Wolf packs' of U-boats attacked convoys crossing the Atlantic, inflicting terrible losses. Skilful U-boat captains could avoid sonar by getting inside the convoy and attacking on the surface at night, when the small outline of the U-boat's conning-tower was almost impossible to see.

A photograph of a merchant ship under attack, taken through a U-boat's periscope. Submarine captains tried to show as little of the periscope as possible, to avoid being spotted by enemy aircraft and warships.

A DEADLY GAME

When they did detect a U-boat, the escorting warships played a deadly game of cat-and-mouse, trying to destroy the submarine or drive it away from the convoy.

Despite great bravery and skill, the U-boats could not win the war at sea. Between 1939 and 1945, 1,162 new U-boats entered service. Of these, only 156 survived the war. All the rest had been sunk, lost by accident or shipwreck, or scuttled - sunk by their own crews rather than surrender to the enemy.

SUPER CARRIERS

Until the 1950s, the 80,000-tonne passenger liners remained the biggest ships ever built. With the coming of nuclear power, these pre-war ships were surpassed by the huge nuclear-powered aircraft carriers of the United States Navy. These great vessels can travel right round the world without refuelling.

An F-14 Tomcat fighter, armed with underwing missiles, is hurled into the air from the bow steam catapult of an American 'Nimitz' class super-carrier.

THE FIRST 'FLAT-TOPS'

The first aircraft carriers appeared at the end of World War 1. Rebuilt from the hulls of large merchant ships and battleships, they were designed with a long flight deck for the aircraft to take off and land on. However, it was not until World War 2 that purpose-built carriers proved their worth as their planes launched devastating attacks on enemy fleets. During the war in the Pacific, Japanese and American carriers fought vast battles without ever seeing the other's ships!

THE *NIMITZ*

More recently, the United States Navy has built the USS *Nimitz* and several sister-ships. These giant nuclear-powered carriers are the biggest warships and the most sophisticated floating structures ever built. (They are surpassed in size only by the oil-carrying super-tankers which displace over 250,000 tonnes when fully loaded.) The super-carriers are floating airfields that enable the US government to 'project' military power all over the world. They are also complicated floating cities, crammed from end to end with high technology, including two nuclear reactors which provide power for at least 13 years (or over a million kilometres of steaming). As a result, they displace just under 93,000 tonnes and have a crew of 6,300 men. 3,000 of these belong to the 'air group' on the ship.

POWER AND GLORY

The carrier's air group operates over 90 aircraft. These include powerful strike aircraft, capable of bombing an enemy's forces by day or night and in nearly all weather. There are also fighters and anti-submarine aircraft for the ship's own protection, 'tankers' that can refuel other aircraft in the air, and even electronic warfare aircraft for jamming enemy radar and detecting attackers.

The heavy jets need long flight decks for take-off and landing. To help them get into the air, giant catapults harness the power of the nuclear reactors and accelerate them to over 100 km per hour in just 3 seconds. After a flight, aircraft are moved from the flight deck to the giant hangars and workshops below using four lifts, called elevators, at the ship's side.

LIFE BELOW DECKS

A super-carrier generates enough electric power to supply a city of two million people, while its crew consumes over 12 tonnes of food a day. Every year the medical department will complete more than 8,000 blood tests and 3,000 medical check-ups. This is a far cry from the ancient Egyptians with their tied-up bundles of reeds!

The scene in the Carrier Air Traffic Control Center (CATCC) of a super-carrier. The constantly-updated information on the screens shows which aircraft have been launched, and which are due for launching or recovery.

Too valuable to sail alone, modern carriers usually operate as part of a battle group. With this carrier are an anti-submarine frigate (upper left) and an anti-aircraft cruiser armed with the AEGIS missile system. AEGIS can engage many targets simultaneously and control a whole fleet's defences. Always in the air are a radar-fitted aircraft to detect low-flying enemy aircraft, and a helicopter for the instant rescue of aircrew in the event of crashes at sea.

Strictly defined, a ship is a sailing vessel with at least three masts. Such craft (with the exception of the giant Chinese junks) did not exist before the 15th century AD, yet sailors had been making ocean voyages for well over 4,000 years before then. This book uses the word 'ship' for vessels able to make cargo-carrying voyages on the open sea. A submarine is any powered vessel capable of diving and returning to the surface.

c2300 BC An Egyptian fleet attacks Syria, the earliest known use of ships in war.
c1000-550 BC Phoenician merchant ships dominate Mediterranean sea trade.
480 BC A Greek trireme fleet defeats Persians at the huge battle of Salamis.
264-241 BC Roman fleets win control of western Mediterranean from Carthage.
30 BC-AD 410 The Roman Empire is served by world's biggest merchant fleet.
c300-900 Pacific islanders in sailing canoes populate central Pacific islands.
c850-1000 Viking explorers reach Iceland, Greenland and North America.
c900-1500 Arab traders reach India, the East Indies and the China coast.

c1480-1500 Portuguese and Spanish caravels open the ocean routes to India and the Americas.
1571 Battle of Lepanto, the last big sea fight between fleets of war galleys.
1588 The Spanish Armada battles, the first sea fights between galleon fleets armed with broadside-mounted cannon.
1808 Fulton's *Phoenix* makes the first sea voyage under steam.
1845 Brunel's *Great Britain* is the first steamship built wholly of iron.
1862 *Merrimack* versus *Monitor*, the first fight between steam-powered 'ironclads'.
1864 *Housatonic* becomes the first warship to be sunk by submarine attack.
c1848-1880 Record sailing voyages by high-speed clippers fail to halt the change from sail to steam.
1916 Battle of Jutland, only big sea fight between fleets of Dreadnought battleships.
1907-39 Pursuing the 'Blue Riband', fast Atlantic passenger liners become the world's biggest ships.
1940-1943 Germany's U-boats are defeated in the Battle of the Atlantic.
1955 USS *Nautilus*, the first nuclear-powered submarine, enters service.
1975 Nuclear-powered carrier *Nimitz*, the biggest warship in history.

Roman soldiers rush from their galley across a corvus, or 'crow', that has been dropped onto an opponent's deck (see also page 8). The large spike on the corvus will hold the ships together. In the background, another oared galley is approaching. In early Greek and Roman times, the job of the rower was considered an honourable one. Later, criminals and slaves were forced to row the galleys.

Glossary

bank: a deck of rowers in a galley.

beam: the width of a ship.

carvel: a shipbuilding technique with the hull planks laid smooth, edge to edge.

clinker: a shipbuilding technique with the hull planks overlapping.

complement: the full number of officers and sailors making up a ship's crew.

convoy: a group of merchant ships sailing together for greater protection.

displacement: a ship's weight, measured by the amount of water pushed aside when the ship is afloat.

galleass: a 16th century warship driven by both sail and oars.

galley: a warship driven by one or more banks of oars; or a ship's kitchen.

jibs: small triangular sails set at the bow of a ship.

junk: a large Chinese sailing ship, from the Portuguese word *junco* (in turn a version of the Javanese *djong*, or 'ship').

lateen sail: a triangular sail perfected by the Arabs and adopted by Europeans or 'Latins' by the 15th century.

poop deck: the small uppermost deck at the stern of a ship.

quarterdeck: a raised deck running from a ship's mainmast to the stern.

tacking: steering a zig-zag course to make progress against the wind.

trireme: a Greek war galley driven by three banks of oars.

wa'a kaulua: 'double canoe' - a large twin-hulled sailing canoe of the Pacific.

Quotations

The words of navigator Mau Piailug were spoken to the crew of *Hokule'a* before their voyage from Hawaii to Tahiti in 1976. 'King Harald's Saga', in praise of Harald Hardraada of Norway, tells of Harald's voyage to Constantinople (Byzantium). Marco Polo's description of Chinese junks comes from his famous travel book, *Description of the World*. Christopher Columbus tells of *Pinta's* historic landfall in the Americas in the journal of his first Atlantic crossing in 1492. Lord Howard of Effingham was the English fleet's commander during the Spanish Armada campaign. He describes how his galleons drove back the Spanish Armada's galleasses off the Isle of Wight.

INDEX